# Will Todd
# Mass in Blue

for soprano solo, SATB,
and piano, bass, drum kit, and
optional alto saxophone

MUSIC DEPARTMENT

OXFORD

UNIVERSITY PRESS

# OXFORD

**UNIVERSITY PRESS**

Great Clarendon Street, Oxford OX2 6DP,
United Kingdom

Oxford University Press is a department of the University of Oxford.
It furthers the University's objective of excellence in research, scholarship,
and education by publishing worldwide. Oxford is a registered trade mark of
Oxford University Press in the UK and in certain other countries

First published 2014

Impression: 14

ISBN 978-0-19-340050-4

Music and text origination by Julia Bovee
Printed in Great Britain on acid-free paper by
Halstan & Co. Ltd, Amersham, Bucks.

# Contents

# Composer's note

*Mass in Blue* came into being as the result of a commission from David Temple and Hertfordshire Chorus in 2003. Musically, it represents a conscious collision of two musical genres which have been a central part of my artistic life for many years: sacred choral music and jazz. It was somewhat daunting to set the Latin mass, so familiar to me from having sung the great settings by Byrd, Haydn, and others, and it took me a while to find my way into the piece and work out what I wanted to say: in the end, plainsong and the 12-bar blues showed me the way forward. I also incorporated several features of Gospel singing: improvisatory solos, choral textures that veer between unison and much richer harmonies, and call-and-response patterns. Since its first performance in 2003 I have been thrilled and gratified to see it take flight and be performed all over the UK and, increasingly, further afield. Its dissemination has certainly been aided by the economic option of the version for jazz trio which was pioneered in Cambridge by my colleague Ralph Woodward and the Fairhaven Singers. I have experienced the piece in a wide variety of guises and venues, sung by choirs of many different types, and I must admit that it still excites me every time—I hope you enjoy it too.

Rhythm section players should feel free to use the chord symbols and to add and improvise texture around the parts.

Duration: *c.*37 minutes

Also available:
Mass in Blue Jazz Trio Set (piano, bass, drum kit, and optional alto sax) (ISBN 978–0–19–340481–6)
Mass in Blue Backing CD (ISBN 978–0–19–340214–0)

A separate, compatible big-band version is also available on hire/rental from Tyalgum Press (contact: info@ tyalgumpress.com).

*Commissioned by David Temple and Hertfordshire Chorus, 2003*

# Mass in Blue

## 1. *Kyrie*

WILL TODD

Printed in Great Britain

OXFORD UNIVERSITY PRESS, MUSIC DEPARTMENT, GREAT CLARENDON STREET, OXFORD OX2 6DP

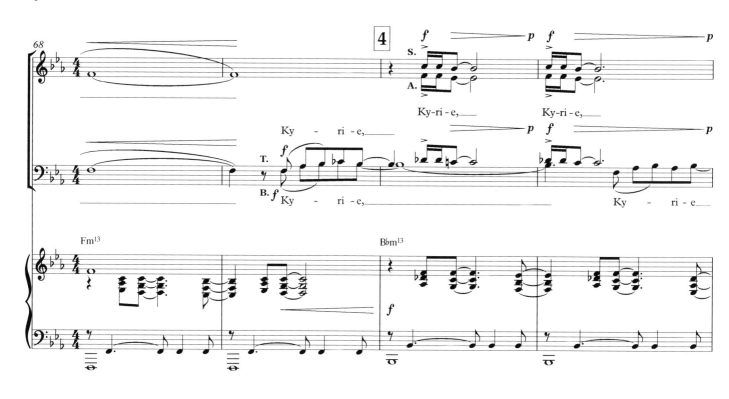

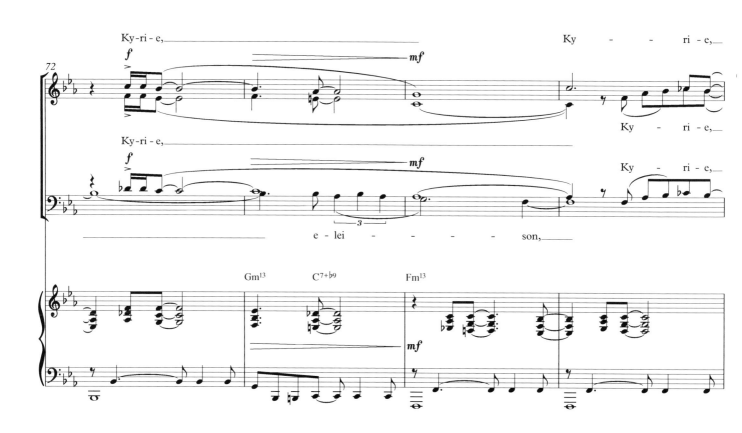

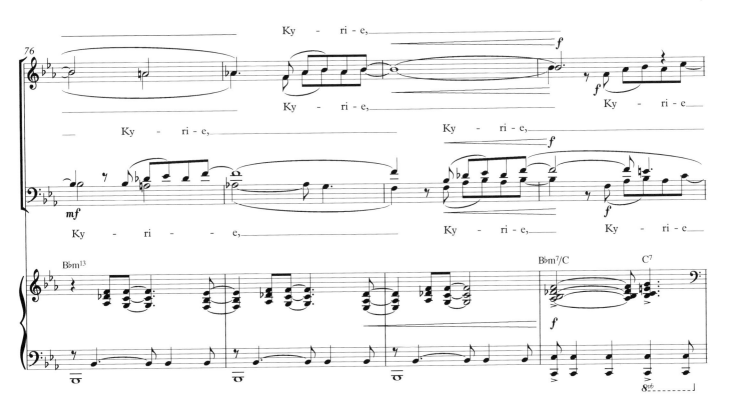

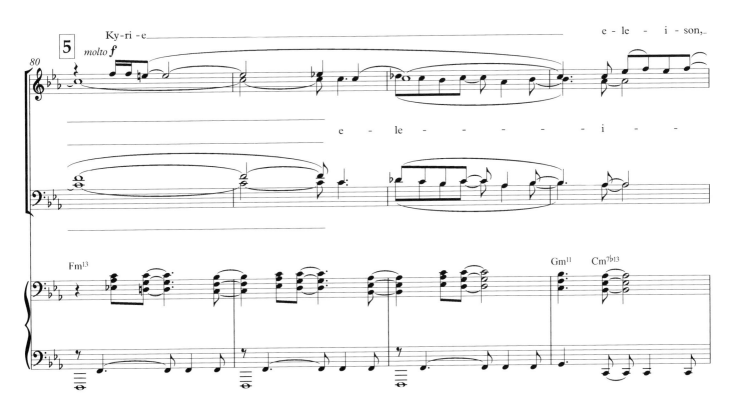

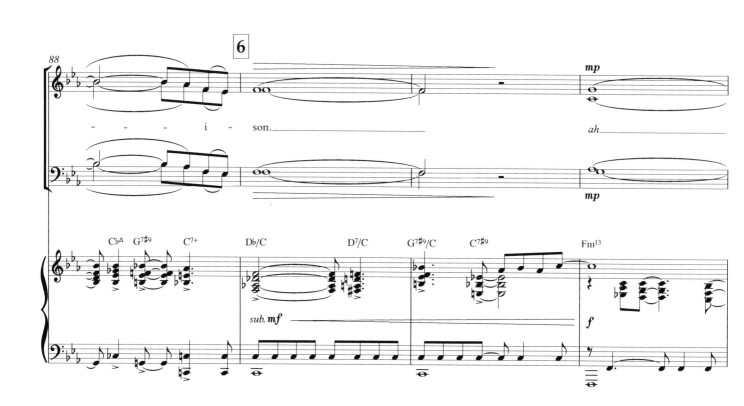

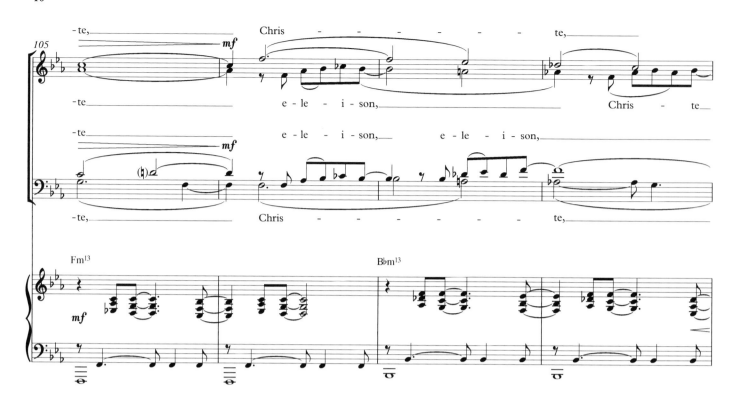

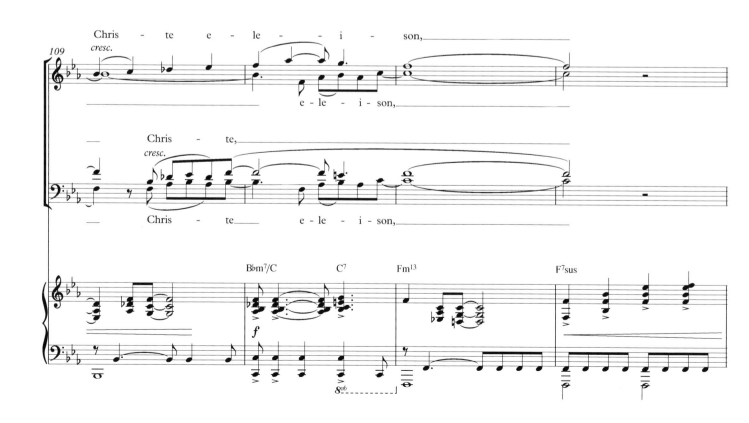

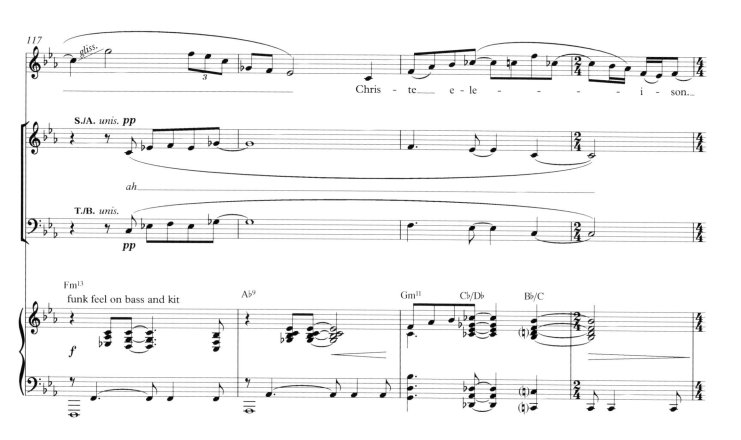

* Cue-sized notes are optional throughout.

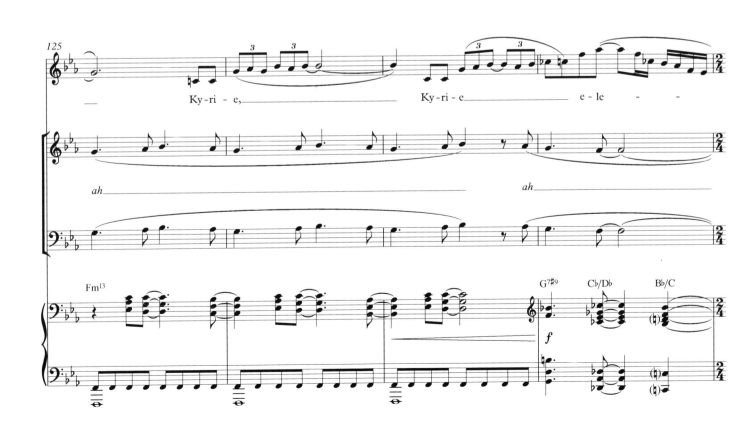

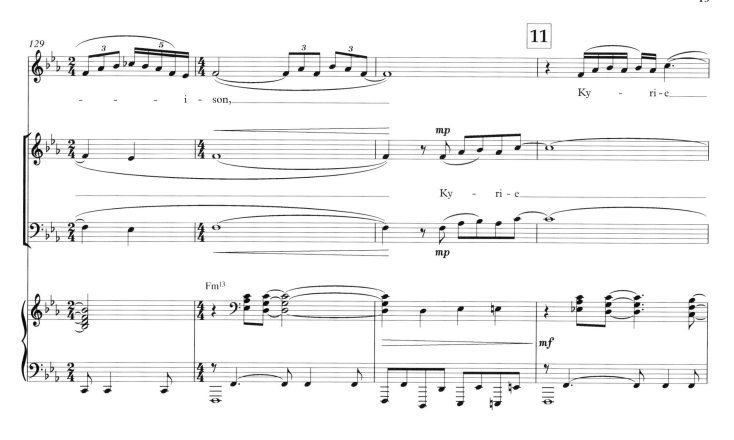

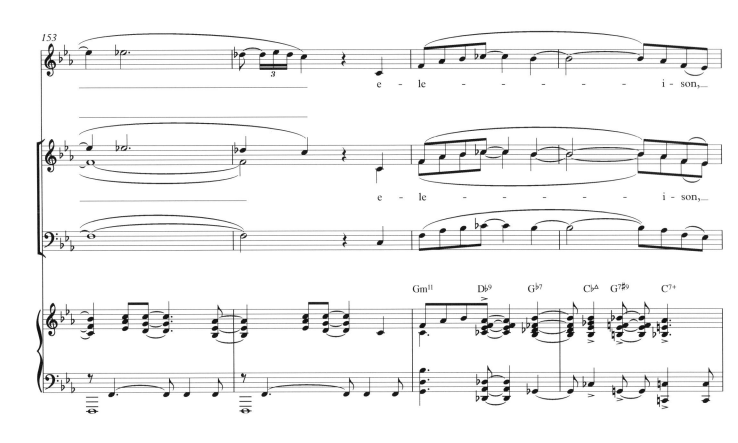

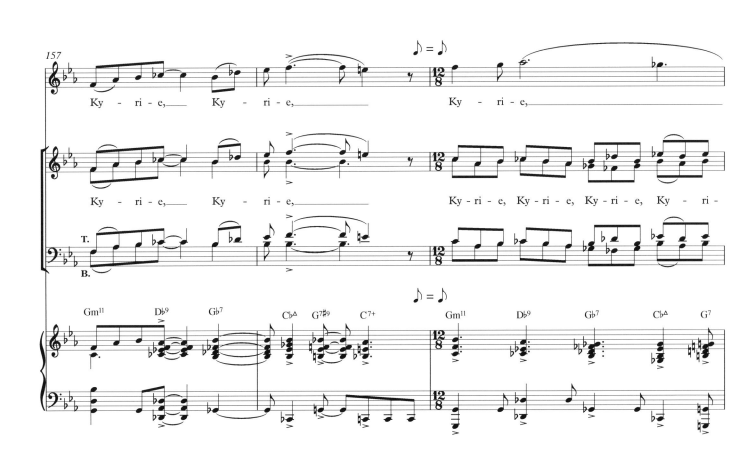

# 2. Gloria

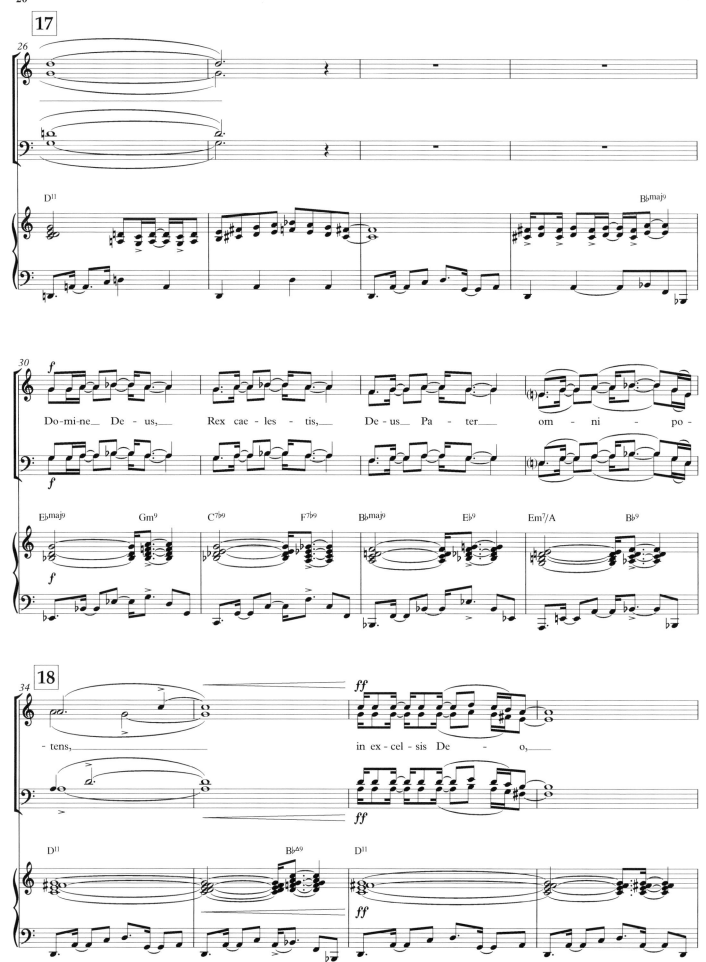

# 3. *Credo*

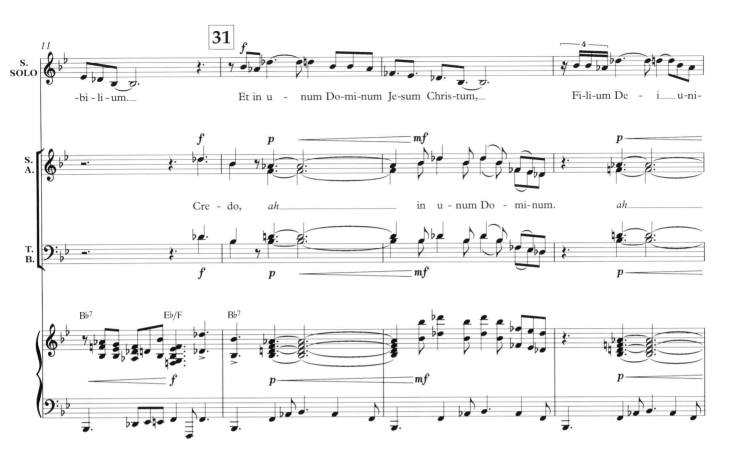

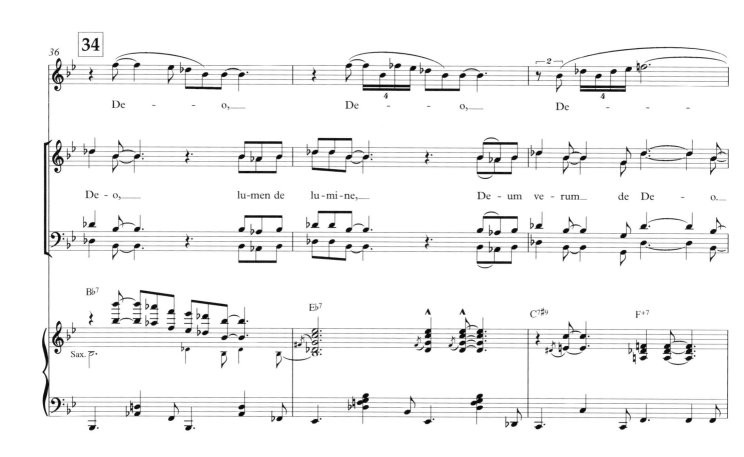

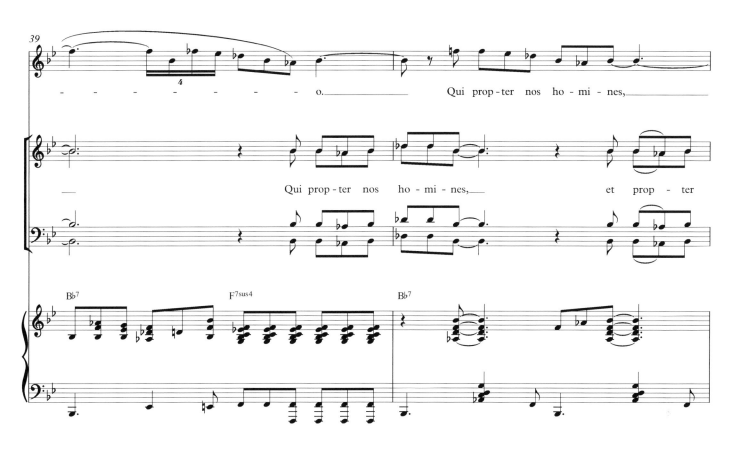

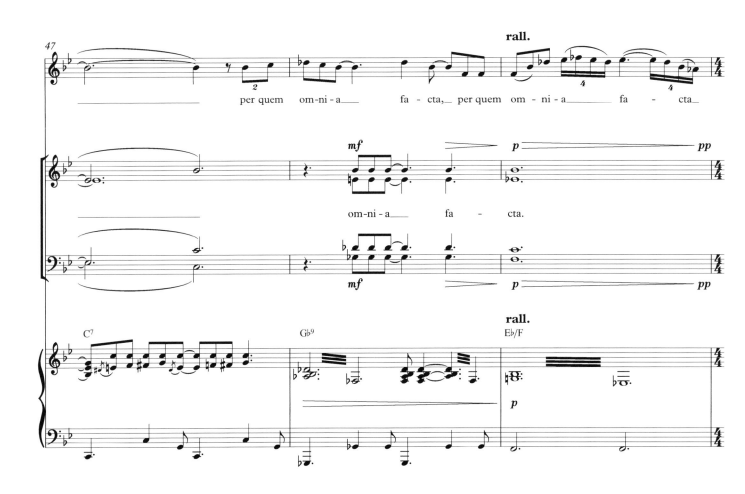

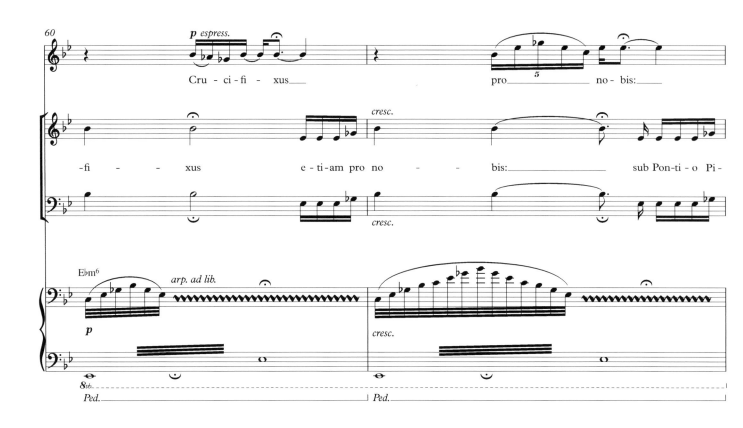

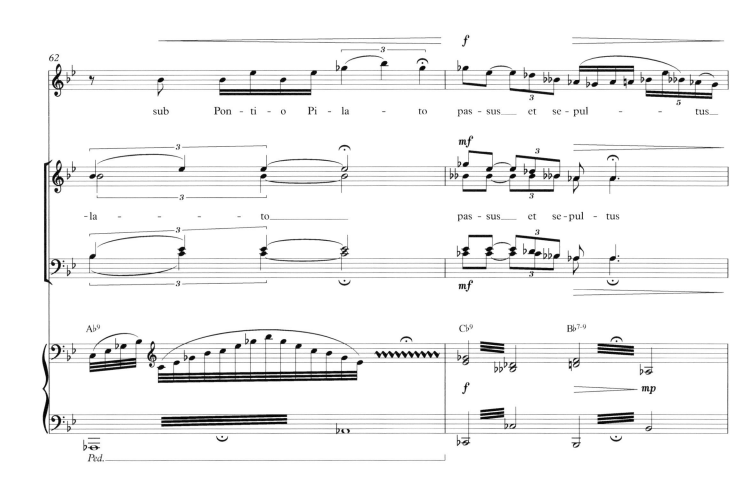

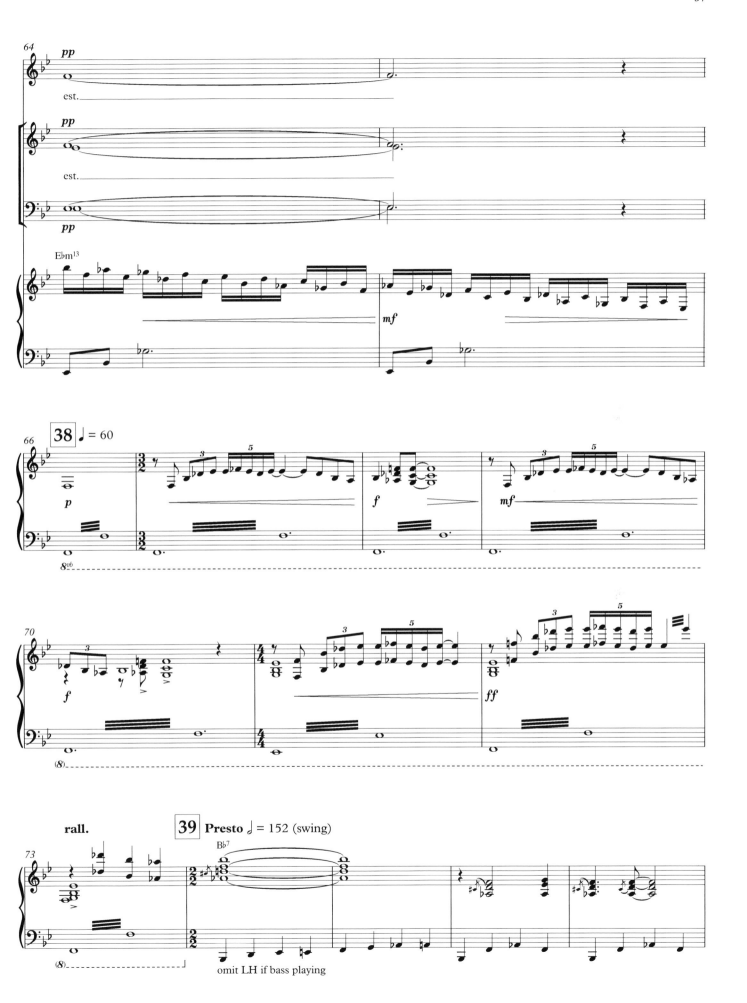

38

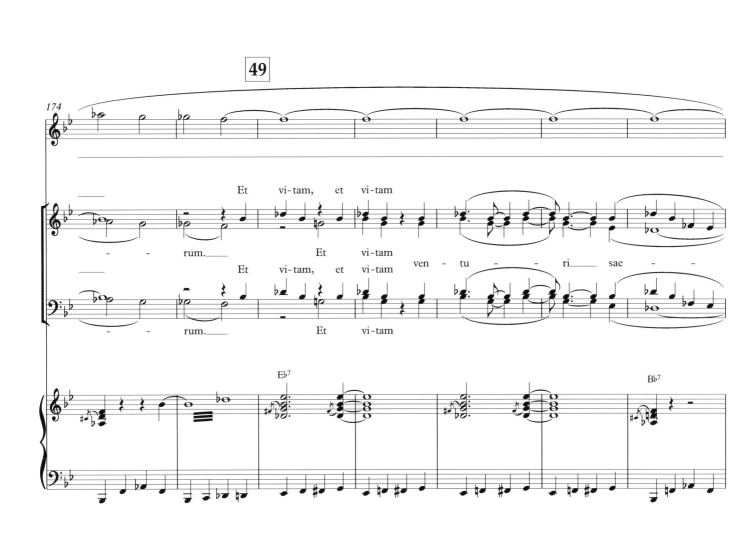

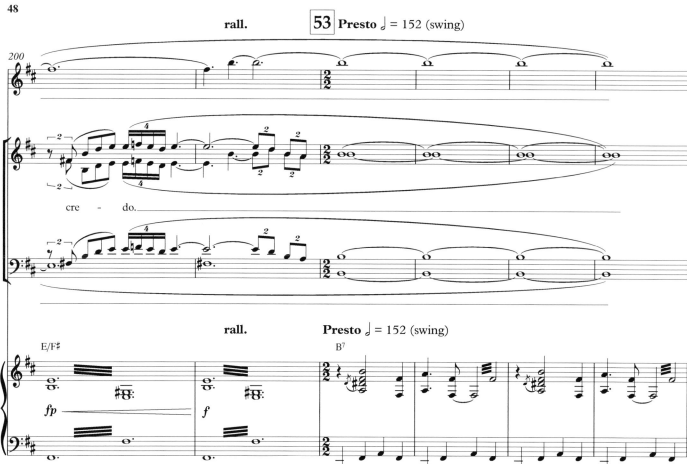

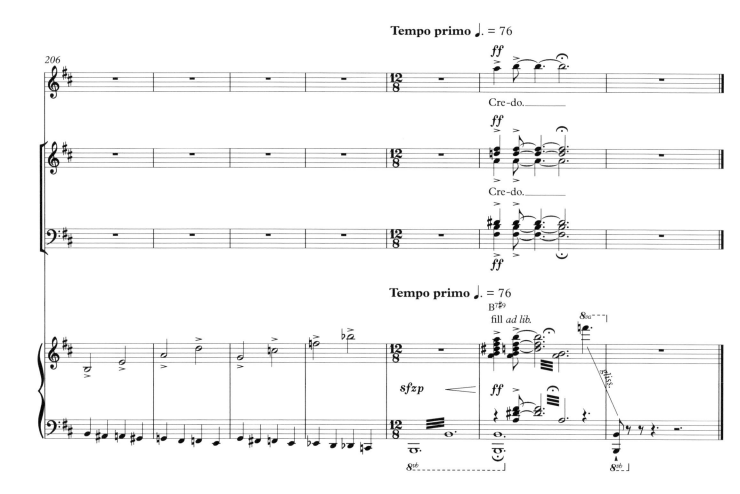

# 4. *Sanctus*

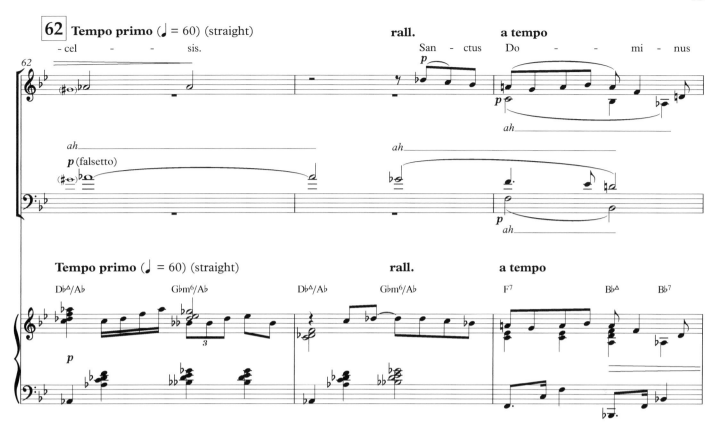

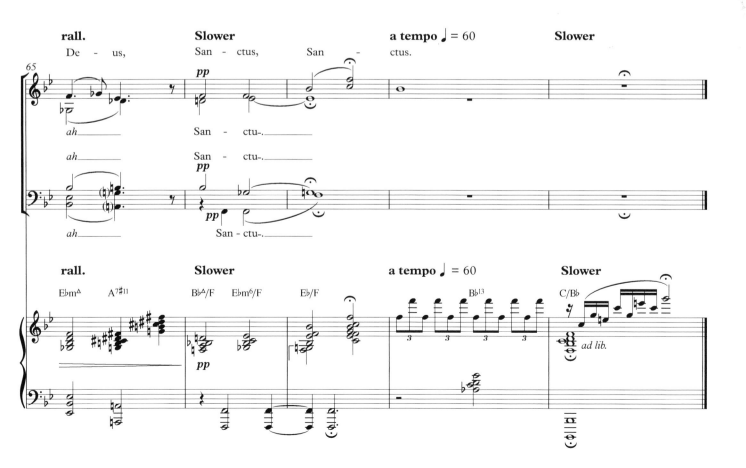

# 5. Benedictus

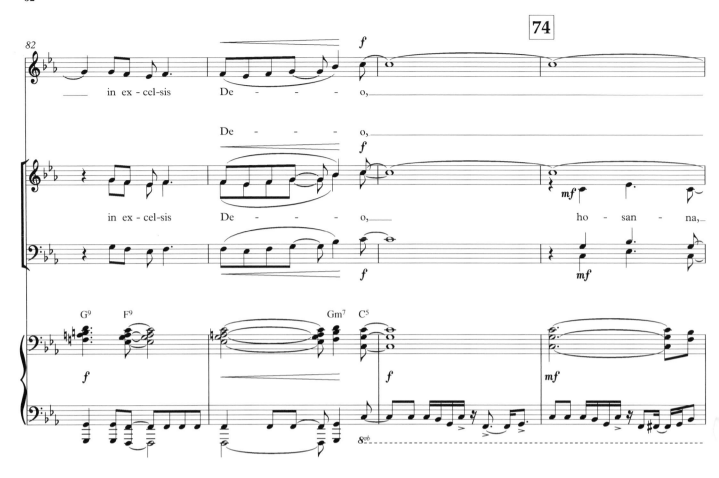

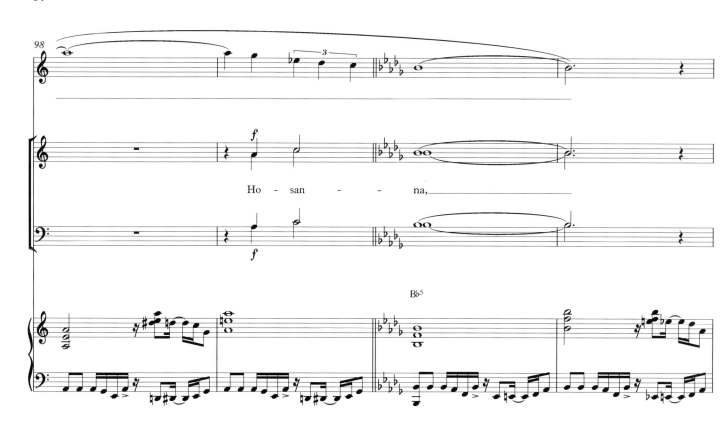

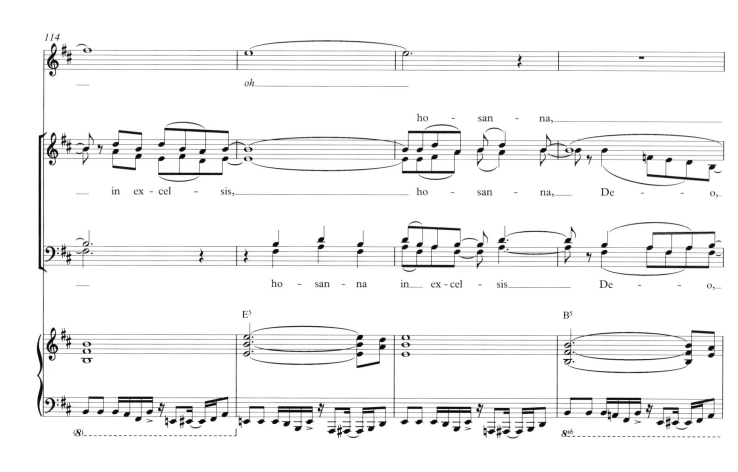

# 6. *Agnus Dei*

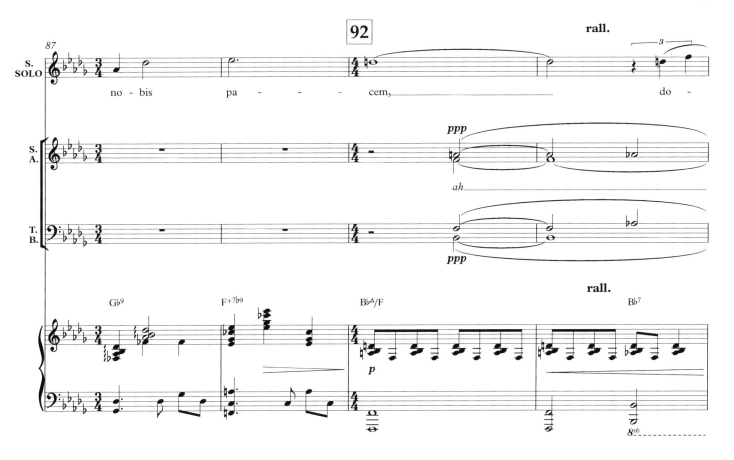

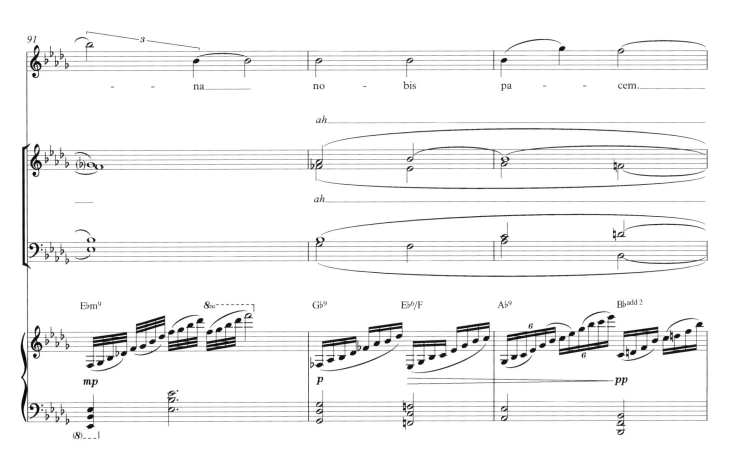

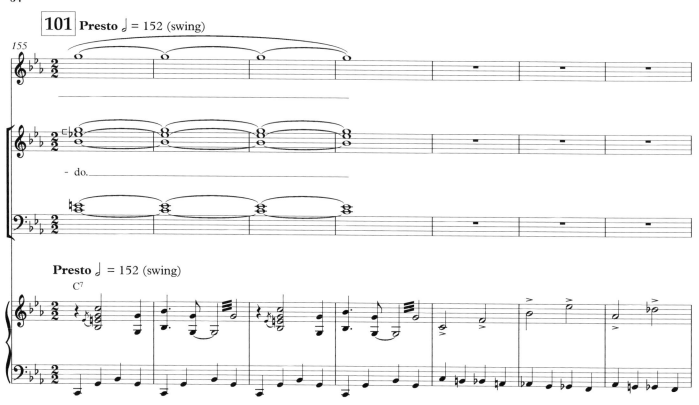

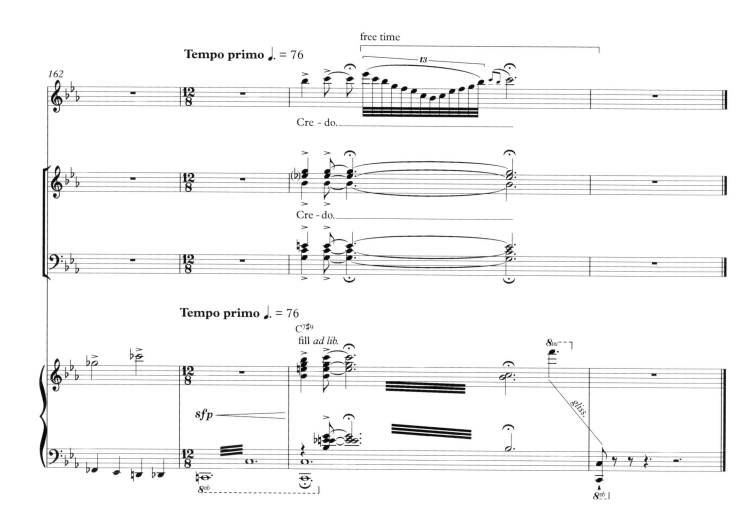